Echoes of her Voice

Saba Masoodi

Qurate
quratebooks.com

Echoes of her Voice

Saba Masoodi

Published in 2024

© Published by

Qurate Books Pvt. Ltd.
Goa 403523, India
www.quratebooks.com
Tel: 1800-210-6527, Email: info@quratebooks.com

ISBN: 978-93-58983-57-9

Introduction

I am Saba Masoodi, an English teacher from the beautiful region of Srinagar, Kashmir.

My book *'Echoes of Her Voice'*, is a heartfelt reflection of my observations and experiences as a woman in the society. It captures the complex realities that many women face, where their voices often go unheard and their self-worth is overlooked.

Through this book, I address the societal expectations that compel women to place the needs of their families and society above their own, often at the expense of their health, peace of mind, and personal growth. I have seen how women are conditioned to remain silent, to prioritize everything but themselves.

This book is my way of urging all women to step out of the shadows and recognize their own strength.

'Echoes of Her Voice' is not just a collection of poetry; it is a call to action. It is for every woman who has felt trapped, silenced, or undervalued. I want to remind you that your life is precious, that you deserve to dream, to fight for those dreams, and to stand up for yourself.

Through my words, I hope to inspire you to break free from the constraints of societal expectations and live authentically and joyfully. This book is my tribute to every woman who is striving to find her voice and assert her identity. I believe that now is the time for all women to reclaim their stories and create lives filled with purpose, joy, and fulfilment.

Let Echoes of Her Voice be your companion on this journey towards self-discovery and empowerment, because this life is yours to live—fully and fearlessly.

Poem 1

In Islam's gentle grace, marriage finds its home,
A sacred bond where mutual respect is sown.
For Allah's order and the Prophet's decree,
We wed to honour, to make them pleased with thee.

Treat with piety, with sincerity deep,
Cruelty to spouses, let us not keep.
The wife, a cherished honour, must be,
Respected, honoured, in harmony.

Yet, in these days, some men assume,
A dominance, a power, a prideful fume.
But Prophet's example, a gentle guide,
Never did he put his wife aside.

And women too, in their own right,
Should not overbear, nor demand in spite.
For the bond of marriage, a sacred trust,
In mutual respect, we find our just.

Some may think to raise a hand,
To strike a wife, a cruel demand.
But Allah's creation, both man and wife,
Are bound in love, not in strife.

Consult, negotiate, in partnership true,
Decisions shared, not just for the few.
For Islam's wisdom, in marriage gleams,
A union of souls, fulfilled in dreams.

Poem 2

In the shadows of a world once bright,
Where dreams should soar, and hearts take flight,
Lies a pain, a burden, a silent plight,
Borne by women through the darkest night.

A symphony of sorrows, a song unsung,
Where every note is a tear that's wrung.
From souls that ache, from hearts that long,
For a world where their voices belong.

In every step, in every stride,
Lies the weight of expectations, hard to abide,
With every breath, with every sigh,
Comes a whispered question: "Why must we try?"

For in this world, where respect should reign,
Where love and care should ease the pain,
Too often, women find disdain,
Their worth diminished, their struggles in vain.

Accused, misunderstood, and torn,
Their spirits bruised, their hopes forlorn,
Yet still they rise, resilient, reborn,
Their strength a beacon, their courage worn.

So let us listen, let us hear,
The echoes of their pain, the silent tear.
Let us stand, side by side, sincere,
In solidarity, till their skies are clear.

For the story of female pain,
Is not just theirs, but ours to gain,
A lesson in empathy, in love's refrain,
A testament to our shared humanity's domain.

Poem 3

In the cradle of her love, we find our birth,
Nine months of sacrifice, the greatest worth.
Through pains endured, her love unfurled,
A mother's bond, the strongest in the world.

From infancy to age, her arms enfold,
In her embrace, we find our stronghold.
Through joys and tears, she guides our way,
Her love, a beacon, come what may.

Her sacrifices, silent and unseen,
Her devotion, unwavering, serene.
With every step, she's by our side,
Her love, an eternal, endless tide.

In moments of triumph, her eyes glisten,
Her pride in us, a love unbroken, listen.
And when the world seems cold and drear,
Her warmth, her love, always near.

She gives her all, without complaint,
Her love, a constant, unwavering saint.
To all the mothers, we sing this praise,
For their love, our eternal daze.

Happy Mother's Day, in every way,
To the mothers who light up our day.
In their love, we find our truest measure,
For they are our eternal treasure.

Poem 4

In the quiet whispers of twilight's embrace,
Lies the essence of love, in maternal grace.
Mothers, the pillars of strength, unwavering and true,
Their love, an ocean, endless and blue.

Yet beside them stand, in the light's gentle sway,
Teachers, guiding stars, lighting our way.
Value them as mothers, for they nurture our minds,
With wisdom's touch, their light forever shines.

Respect your mother, in her embrace find solace,
Before time's cruel hand leads to its grim palace.
Cherish her, love her, let your trust be unfurled,
For her love, the most precious gem in this world.

And to your teacher, extend the same grace,
For their guidance shapes futures, in time and space.
In their lessons, find blessings, for they pave the way,
To dreams realized, in the light of day.

As age unfurls its tapestry, and time slips away,
We'll yearn for their presence, in moments astray.
For their guidance, a beacon, in life's ebb and flow,
In their wisdom, seeds of greatness they sow.

Honored by Allah, in their love find worth,
For their blessings, the most precious of Earth.
So bow to your mother, bow to your teacher's care,
Respect, value, before life's curtain you dare to tear.

Poem 5

In the dance of life, hand in hand we stride,
Through highs and lows, together we abide.
Communication, the first step on this road,
Speaking our hearts, easing each other's load.

Trust, a sturdy bridge we construct,
Built with honesty, never to be destructed.
In the mosaic of time, make moments to share,
For in each other's company, love blossoms rare.

Leave behind the shadows of yesterday's pain,
In the present, our love shall eternally reign.
Arguments may arise, storms may brew,
But through it all, our bond stays true.

Flaws are but facets of our uniqueness to see,
In acceptance lies the key to harmony.
Let's be not just lovers, but the best of friends,
With a love that transcends, never bends.

In the garden of our marriage, let love bloom,
With every heartbeat, dispelling all gloom.
For in the symphony of our souls, we find,
A love, pure and unconditional, forever intertwined.

Poem 6

In the fabric of society, she weaves her grace,
A woman, a mother, in every embrace.
Her strength unmatched, her spirit unbound,
Yet shackled by norms, in silence, she's found.

In every step, she carries the weight,
Yet her voice suppressed, silenced by hate.
She's not just a day, but a yearlong song,
Of resilience and power, steady and strong.

In marriages failed, blame falls on her name,
While men walk away, untouched by the blame.
Leading a society, she's labeled a curse,
Yet she builds the world, with every verse.

Friendships restricted, boundaries set,
But why should her choices cause such regret?
In every decision, she's labeled a threat,
For daring to rise, society's bet.

But she's more than just roles, more than just names,
In her essence, lies the world's flames.
A woman, a force, unyielding and true,
Deserves respect, in all that she'll do.

So let's break the chains, let's pave the way,
For every woman, every single day.
For she's not just a day, she's eternity's play,
In her strength and her glory, let's find our way.

Poem 7

In the dance of time, each second a fresh start,
Every hour whispers secrets to the heart.
In the night's embrace, dreams weave their spell,
And each day's canvas, ours alone to dwell.

Let go, they say, of burdens past,
For today's pain, tomorrow's strength amassed.
A choice presented, to turn or to close,
In the book of life, a new chapter arose.

Embrace the now, seize the day,
Life's passage ours, to pave the way.
From within, rebuild, love unbound,
Emotions released, in solitude found.

Walk alone, beneath the sky's expanse,
Live within means, let not greed enhance.
Nurture strength within, let it bloom,
Apologies shed, in self, find room.

Surround with light, positive and bright,
Embrace the moment, day or night.
For in every ending, a new start we borrow,
A new beginning, a hopeful tomorrow.

Poem 8

To find love that's pure and true,
One must embody virtues too.
For in the dance of hearts, we find,
Reflections of our own design.

A good man seeks a goodly soul,
Whose essence makes his spirit whole.
So too, a woman's heart shall see,
The goodness in a man set free.

Be kind, be true, in word and deed,
In every thought, plant love's seed.
For what we give, we shall receive,
In love's embrace, we find reprieve.

So strive to be the best you can,
In every moment, every plan.
For in the end, it's understood,
To find true love, be truly good.

Poem 9

In Sujud's embrace, tears silently fall,
Yet before the world, she stands tall.
Do you know her? The woman of grace,
With patience deeper than time's embrace.

In her tears, a prayer's whispered plea,
In her smile, strength for all to see.
She bears the weight of trials untold,
With patience, her heart's fortress bold.

Through every storm, she finds her way,
In the darkest night, she finds the day.
For she knows in patience lies the key,
To unlock the door to serenity.

So honour her, the woman with sabr,
In her silence, the loudest stir.
For in her tears and in her smile,
Resides the beauty of trials' trial.

Poem 10

In the tapestry of life, threads come undone,
Sometimes, dear woman, partings do come.
Allah's wisdom, a mysterious sight,
In every loss, a pathway to light.

Look not behind, but forward, dear friend,
For in every ending, new beginnings blend.
Trust in the plan, though it may seem unclear,
The future awaits, devoid of fear.

With faith as your guide, and hope as your song,
March forth with courage, steadfast and strong.
For what's meant to be will find its way,
In Allah's grace, let your heart sway.

So remember, dear woman, in Allah's decree,
Each parting serves a purpose, a key.
Embrace the journey, let go of the past,
For in the future's embrace, love will last.

Poem 11

In the heart of a woman, tender and true,
Lives a fragility known to few.
With a soul so soft, like petals of a rose,
Innocence in her, constantly grows.

She needs care, like the morning dew,
Gentle hands to hold her through.
She needs love, like a bird needs flight,
A guiding star in the darkest night.

From her man, she seeks a shield,
A fortress strong, a loving field.
The man who is hers, destined to stay,
To guard her heart, come what may.

The man she'll marry, steadfast and kind,
Who sees the beauty in her mind.
Who stands with her in joy and pain,
Like Sun and Earth, in endless reign.

For women are fragile, soft at heart,
A mosaic of love, each delicate part.
Full of care, in every glance,
In her pure, innocent dance.

She needs a man who understands,
The gentle ways of love's demands.
To cherish her, to hold her near,
To be her strength, her partner dear.

For in her fragility lies her grace,
A tender touch, a loving embrace.
She needs a man who'll always be,
Her anchor in the stormy sea.

Poem 12

In twilight's hush, where dreams begin to weave,
A whisper soft as sighs, your name I breathe.
Stars above, like diamonds in the night,
Reflect the fire within your eyes so bright.

Your laughter, music sweet, a melody,
That dances through my heart, sets it free.
In every touch, your gentle warmth I find,
A solace deep, in love our souls entwined.

Your grace, a river flowing smooth and clear,
Carries me through days, both far and near.
With every glance, a promise you impart,
A vow unspoken, sealed within my heart.

The world may change, and seasons come and go,
Yet our love's flame will ever brightly glow.
For in your eyes, I see eternity,
A boundless love that spans infinity.

So take my hand, together we shall roam,
For in your arms, I've found my one true home.
A love profound, a timeless, endless art,
Forever etched within my heart.

Poem 13

He whispers, "I love you," soft as a breeze,
Yet she hears only words, no feeling to seize.
His voice, a melody, sweet and sincere,
But love's touch and thrill, she cannot hear.

Love, a dance of heartbeats, felt deep within,
A symphony of senses, where true love begins.
Yet in her world, it remains just a sound,
A hollow echo, where no warmth is found.

Love craves to be felt, to be touched, to be known,
Not merely in words, but through actions shown.
It's a spark, a thrill, an unspoken connection,
A profound attachment, a shared affection.

To love is to show, in every gesture and glance,
A tender caress, a passionate dance.
For love isn't just spoken, it's meant to be seen,
In the silent moments, where true love convenes.

So let not love linger as mere whispered air,
But let it be felt, in moments we share.
For love in its essence is more than a word,
It's a vivid feeling, in every heart stirred.

Poem 14

I read a quote that made me pause,
To see the world and question flaws.
"My life improved," it boldly said,
"When niceness from my life had fled."

For being nice had left me bruised,
Used, stressed out, and oft abused.
But goodness, true, was something more,
A strength, a heart, a deeper core.

You don't need niceness to be kind,
True goodness speaks with mind aligned.
It sets firm boundaries, honest and clear,
Without the weight of guilt or fear.

Being good means self-respect,
Values strong, no need to deflect.
Niceness may win fleeting praise,
But seldom does it truly raise.

To be good is to honor your soul,
With truth and courage as your goal.
Temporary smiles may fade away,
But respect and love, in goodness, stay.

So cherish truth, let it be your guide,
In its light, no need to hide.
For in the end, you will see,
Being good is the way to be free.

Poem 15

In someone's story, we all play the foe,
A role we can't alter, a fate we can't tow.
Perspectives vary, like shadows at dusk,
But self-respect is a duty we must trust.

We can't shift the lens through which others see,
Nor rewrite the chapters in their memory.
But steadfast we stand, in our truth and our might,
Holding our values, our sense of what's right.

Expectations from others may falter and fade,
Yet our own respect must never be swayed.
In the mirror's reflection, let honor be clear,
A beacon of strength, unwavering and dear.

For in the end, what truly holds weight,
Is the respect for ourselves, we cultivate.
Let them think as they may, their judgments unknown,
We walk our own path, in self-respect, alone.

Poem 16

In the quiet dawn of morning's light,
A woman's heart shines pure and bright.
Her love is deep, her spirit strong,
In her, a melody, a timeless song.

If you nourish her with tender care,
You'll find her love is always there.
Take care of her thoughts, let them be free,
For in her mind, dreams are the key.

Her smile, a beacon, warm and true,
Cherish it, and it will shine for you.
When tears fall softly from her eyes,
Wipe them gently, soothe her sighs.

Respect her essence, her inner grace,
Honour the soul within her embrace.
In her silence, a story untold,
Listen closely, let her unfold.

Her happiness is a delicate flower,
Guard it closely, every hour.
Ensure her safety, her peace of mind,
In your arms, let comfort she find.

Celebrate her unique personality,
Her quirks, her strengths, her individuality.
Her well-being, your priority,
For in her health, love's purity.

Her life, a tapestry of dreams and hope,
In its threads, with love, you'll cope.
If you take care of her in every way,
Her heart will love you, come what may.

She will love you as no one can,
With a depth unknown to any man.
Her love is boundless, infinite, and true,
A precious gift, she'll give to you.

In the warmth of her embrace,
You'll find your perfect, sacred place.
Her love will lift you, set you free,
A bond so strong, eternally.

No love compares, none can surpass,
The steadfast love of a woman, so vast.
Nourish her, care for her, and you will see,
The depth of her love, a boundless sea.

Poem 17

In the heart of a woman, love abounds,
When nurtured with care, its beauty astounds.
Take care of her thoughts, her dreams, her fears,
And witness her joy, through smiles and tears.

Respect her essence, honour her grace,
Cherish her silence, in its quiet embrace.
Guard her happiness, her safety, her peace,
And see how her love will never cease.

Support her well-being, her life, her mind,
With a gentle touch, be tender and kind.
For if you care for her in every way,
Her love will shine, like the light of day.

No love compares, none can surpass,
The depth of her love, steadfast and vast.
She'll love you truly, with all her heart,
A bond so deep, it won't fall apart.

Poem 18

To those who think we always need men,
For love, for care, for support—
Know this: we may need you then,
But mistreat us, and we'll cut you short.

We are strong, we are bold,
We handle life, we face the storm.
In our arms, our children we hold,
Independent, we transform.

In this century, our strength shines bright,
We hold positions of power and grace.
You cannot break us, day or night,
We carve our own space.

Taunts for lacking a man?
We laugh and move on with pride.
For in our hearts, we know we can,
Achieve much with no one by our side.

We are women, resilient and true,
Countless things we achieve alone.
In a world that often misunderstands,
We stand strong, on our own.

Poem 19

In the depths of my heart, pain resides,
A burden unseen, a sorrow that hides.
No one can feel, no one can heal,
Except Allah, the wounds concealed.

The pain within, no touch can trace,
An echo of loss, in a silent space.
Forever it lingers, this ache I bear,
I miss the life, the joy I used to wear.

Once I smiled, once I was free,
Excitement and courage defined me.
Now I mourn the person I was,
The spirit, the drive, the endless cause.

I was strong, ready to embrace,
Every challenge, every race.
Hard work and tasks, I did not shun,
But life has changed, and now I'm undone.

Upside down, my world now spins,
A constant shadow where light begins.
I miss the old me, the one so bold,
Now in pain, my story is told.

There's so much inside, so much to share,
But no one feels, no one is there.
I am in pain, I cry in vain,
My heart echoes, "I am in pain."

Poem 20

In silence, I dwell, a heart torn apart,
A burden I carry, a weight on this heart.
My soul is shattered, my spirit in chains,
I cry in the shadows, alone in my pain.

Betrayed in this place, once a haven, now cold,
I'm lost in the echoes of lies left untold.
For my parents, my brothers, I cling to this life,
To spare them the sorrow, to shield them from strife.

But inside, I'm broken, no light to be found,
I'm drowning in darkness, no voice, not a sound.
I hate what's around me, the silence, the dread,
But the tears are my secret, in my soul, I am dead.

Yet I hide all this torment, keep it deep within,
For those whom I love, I won't let them in.
So I bear this alone, with no one to share,
A hollow existence, a silent despair.

Poem 21

In the heart of a woman, soft as spring's first bloom,
Dwells a tenderness that dances in every room.
She whispers to the winds, and they sing her lullabies,
In the arms of nature, she finds her place, she lies.

Fragile as the morning dew on a petal's edge,
Yet within her, mountains move, she makes a pledge.
To stand tall amidst the storms that shake her core,
She bends but never breaks, always seeking more.

Her strength is like the roots that hold the Earth,
Invisible, profound, beyond her gentle mirth.
Emotions like rivers, they flow, they swell,
In every tear, a story she'll never tell.

She is magic, woven in the fabric of time,
In every smile, in every silent rhyme.
Though she may falter, in her heart is a flame,
A woman, soft yet strong, forever the same.

Poem 22

In a world that once whispered, "You need a man,"
She was told to follow, not to lead, but to stand.
Her voice was hushed, her dreams put on hold,
In a cage of tradition, her story was foretold.

Yet within her heart, a fire fiercely burned,
A yearning for freedom, for a life well-earned.
She learned to rise, to walk on her own,
To build a path, to claim a throne.

She's a doctor, a lawyer, a teacher, a guide,
An engineer, an entrepreneur, with nothing to hide.
She's the keeper of homes, the soul of a place,
With strength in her hands and grace in her face.

No longer confined to shadows or chains,
She's writing her story, breaking the reins.
For every step forward, she honors her voice,
In a world where she stands, by her own choice.

She's more than a role, more than a wife,
She's the architect of her own life.
Salute to the woman who dares to be free,
Who speaks her truth, and dreams endlessly.

She doesn't need permission to spread her wings,
In the symphony of life, she boldly sings.
A woman's right to grow, to work, to thrive,
In her own power, she's truly alive.

Poem 23

She rises with the dawn, her feet upon the floor,
A quiet strength that echoes through every open door.
In the heart of the home, she silently weaves,
A tapestry of care, of hopes, and of dreams.

She tends to the children, the husband, the kin,
A guardian of love, where life's threads begin.
She cooks, she cleans, she mends with grace,
A selfless devotion written on her face.

Yet in the shadows, her worth is sometimes lost,
Her endless toil dismissed as just the cost.
But in truth, she's the glue that holds it all tight,
The invisible force that makes everything right.

She's the warmth in the hearth, the calm in the storm,
A lighthouse that guides, keeping everyone warm.
With hands that heal and a heart that forgives,
She breathes life into the home, where each family member lives.

Though uncelebrated, her role is profound,
She's the rhythm of life, the Earth's steady ground.
For every meal she cooks, for every tear she dries,
In her silent sacrifice, a true hero lies.

So salute the housewife, the queen of the hearth,
For she carries the world in the bend of her arch.
She deserves all the praise, the honor, the love,
For she is the heartbeat, the soul from above.

In her steadfast presence, families grow and thrive,
She's the pulse of the home, keeping everyone alive.
So let's raise her high, where she belongs,
For in her, we find where the heart truly longs

Poem 24

She walks, but shadows loom too close,
Eyes that pry, and whispers that boast.
Her body judged, her steps restrained,
A world unfair, where she's unfairly blamed.

She's not for sale, not yours to claim,
Not public property, nor a name in shame.
Yet hands reach out, unasked, unkind,
As if her worth were theirs to find.

But no more silence, no more fear,
The time for change is drawing near.
Together we'll rise, demand what's right,
For every woman, a fairer fight.

Let's teach respect, let dignity reign,
In streets, in hearts, remove the stain.
Of blaming her for what she wears,
Of treating her as if no one cares.

With hands joined tight, let's stand as one,
A safer world, for daughters, begun.
Equality and justice, our shared goal,
A brighter future, where all are whole.

Poem 25

Ma and Pa, with trembling hands,
Packed my dreams, as time expands.
Each fold of fabric, a silent plea,
Yet what awaits, is my new destiny.

Oh, brother dear, goodbyes are near,
And in your eyes, I see the tear.
A sister's love, forever true,
How my heart aches, saying adieu.

You cherished me, a doll so sweet,
A bond that time can't ever defeat.
In every laugh, in every game,
You kept me safe, you knew my name.

But now, a journey calls me far,
To new horizons, a shining star.
Yet as I go, I carry you,
In every step, in all I do.

So long, my brother, parting's due,
But never doubt, I'll cherish you.
In this new chapter, love will bloom,
But home with you, forever looms.

Poem 26

Rise, O woman, with the dawn in your eyes,
A force of nature, beneath boundless skies.
The world once whispered, but now it roars,
For you've unlocked a thousand doors.

Your strength, resilient as mountains high,
Your voice, a truth none can deny.
You stand, unshaken by winds of doubt,
In silence or in shout, you live out loud.

Today, like yesterday, you claim your space,
Every single day, you shape your place.
Not in shadows, nor behind,
But forward, fierce, and unconfined.

For in your hands, the future grows,
With every dream that in you flows.
You teach, you lead, you rise, you fight—
A beacon of unwavering light.

To every woman, near and far,
A warrior, a queen, a rising star—
Empowered not just for today's sway,
But for every single day.

Poem 27

You can't bring down a woman
Who has learned to walk alone.
Her steps may falter, she may fall,
But strength is in her bones.

When life knocks her to the ground,
She rises, fierce and bold.
For every scar and every bruise,
Are stories yet untold.

She may stumble, she may sway,
But never will she break,
For in her heart, a fire burns,
With every breath she takes.

So let the winds howl and storms rage on,
She's weathered them before.
Each fall just makes her rise again,
Much stronger than before.

Poem 28

Have you ever asked a girl,
Of the secrets her heart keeps?
Behind her smiles and quiet grace,
A world of feelings sleeps.

She hides her love, tucks it away,
To save a bond so dear,
Afraid that one confession
Might make the friendship disappear.

She waits in silent patience,
For a love that may never be.
Yet her heart remains loyal,
Bound by hope's fragile plea.

She knows he may never be hers,
Yet still, she dreams and stays,
For the magic of her love endures,
In a thousand unseen ways.

That's how magical a girl can be,
A quiet, endless tide,
Loyal to her one-sided love,
With strength she holds inside.

Poem 29

Have you ever looked in her eyes,
And wondered what they hide?
A thousand dreams, a sea of hope,
A storm she holds inside.

She guards her heart with laughter,
To keep a friendship whole,
Swallowing her love in silence,
To protect what matters most.

She'll wait a lifetime, if she must,
For the love that isn't hers,
Loyal to a one-sided dream,
No matter how it burns.

She may never speak her feelings,
Nor show what's deep within,
For in her quiet sacrifice,
Her strength will always win.

A girl, so magical and pure,
Carries love within her sighs,
Unseen, unheard, yet always true,
A light that never dies.

Poem 30

You can't bring down a woman
Who walks her path alone.
Her strength is carved from battles,
Her heart, a steel-stone.

She may stumble on her journey,
Fall beneath the weight,
But each time she rises higher,
Carrying more than fate.

Bruised but never broken,
She learns with every fall,
That courage isn't in standing tall,
But in getting up at all.

So let the world throw its darkness,
Its storms, its endless night.
She'll gather every shattered piece,
And turn them into light.

Stronger with every struggle,
Braver with every tear,
She's the woman who walks alone,
And grows mightier year by year.

Poem 31

When you see her, shining bright,
Chasing dreams, embracing light,
Working hard on goals she's set,
Becoming her best self yet—

Pause before you cross her way,
Think of what you're here to say.
Don't interrupt her steady climb,
Unless you bring value, not just time.

Her journey's hers, fierce and true,
Built with strength, she always knew.
So if you're here, make sure you lift,
Her dreams deserve a worthy gift.

For a woman growing, wild and free,
Needs no anchor, no sympathy.
Only join if you bring her grace,
Or let her rise, at her own pace.

Poem 32

Don't just be the girl with a pretty face,
Be the woman of power, of grit, of grace.
Let your beauty shine, but let them see,
There's so much more to who you can be.

Be the mind that questions, the heart that strives,
The strength that builds a life that thrives.
Gather your dreams, go chase them all,
Rise with courage, stand proud, stand tall.

Earn your place, build your own throne,
Be the force they can't dethrone.
With beauty, brains, and wealth combined,
Show the world what power looks like, refined.

Be fierce, be bold, be wise, be kind,
A woman with everything, a limitless mind.
Independent, strong, a queen in her right,
Unshakable, unstoppable, blazing with light.

Poem 33

Fall in love with your life, let it unfold,
In every sunrise, in stories untold.
Wake up early, greet the day,
Breathe in the morning, chase dreams away.

Buy your favorite coffee, savor each sip,
Feel the warmth, let it dance on your lips.
Let every flavor, each drop, each taste,
Remind you that joy is never a waste.

Go for a walk as the world comes alive,
Listen to birds, watch nature thrive.
Feel the Earth beneath your feet,
Every step a rhythm, every breath sweet.

Eat good food, nourish your soul,
Savor each bite, make your plate whole.
Choose what you love, let flavors collide,
In these simple pleasures, let happiness reside.

Dress in the clothes that make you feel strong,
Wear what makes you confident, where you belong.
Let colors and fabrics tell who you are,
A masterpiece walking, your own guiding star.

Listen to music that sets your heart free,
Dance with the wind, let go, just be.
Sing every word, let melodies flow,
In those beats and rhythms, feel life's glow.

Create small moments that light up your day,
In quietness, in laughter, in work, in play.
Watch sunsets paint the sky with fire,
Or stargaze at night, let your soul inspire.

So fall in love with the life that you build,
With every joy, every moment fulfilled.
It's in these little things, where magic thrives,
Purposefully woven into the fabric of your life.

Smile at strangers, embrace what is near,
Celebrate your journey, both far and here.
For life is a collection of moments you choose,
To live with passion, with love, and refuse to lose.

Wake up and feel the beauty of now,
Each day a gift, so take a bow.
Fall in love with your life, and make it your art,
For it's in these small joys that you'll find your heart.

Poem 34

Fall in love with each sunrise glow,
Sip your coffee, take it slow.
Walk through mornings, breathe them in,
Wear what sparks your soul within.

Savor meals, taste joy anew,
Play the songs that speak to you.
In every small and simple way,
Create the magic in each day.

Chase your dreams, let laughter flow,
Make life the love you'll always know.

Poem 35

The most wonderful moment unfolds,
When a woman's spirit bravely molds.
She sees the truth in her own light,
Realizing she holds her own might.

No longer bound by others' say,
No need for permission, come what may.
She lives her truth, her heart unchained,
In her freedom, joy is unrestrained.

She dances to her own heart's song,
In her own rhythm, where she belongs.
It's in this truth that beauty's found,
In living life, unbound, unbound.

Poem 36

To all the women who've fought with grace,
Who've weathered storms and braved the chase,
Sending soft energy, warm and true,
To honor the strength inside of you.

You've borne the weight of every day,
Through trials that kept your spirit at bay.
Strong and tough, you've carved your way,
In the harshest light and darkest day.

You've battled through with grit and might,
Survived the cold, endured the fight.
Yet beneath the armor, soft and real,
Is a heart that longs to simply feel.

You've learned to stand when others fall,
To rise again when shadows call.
But now, it's time to gently flow,
To embrace the peace you've yet to know.

Let the strength you've shown become a breeze,
A soothing whisper through the trees.
Let your spirit, once forged in fire,
Now find its rest, its calm, its desire.

You deserve to glide through each soft dawn,
To let your worries be gently withdrawn.
To live with joy, with grace unbound,
In a world where peace and love are found.

So here's to you, the warriors of old,
May your new journey be kind and bold.
May you flow through life with ease and light,
And find your heart in the softest night.

Poem 37

Anger is the voice that speaks within,
A fierce, unwavering, deep-set din.
It rises from the core of you,
A force that knows what you've been through.

It's not a foe but a lover's guide,
A sentinel by your side.
It senses when you've been betrayed,
When respect and care start to fade.

When mistreatment shadows every day,
When your worth is cast away,
Anger's flame ignites a spark,
A signal that you need to embark.

To step away from what drags you low,
To move from places where your spirit won't grow.
It whispers of the need to change,
To leave behind the old, the strange.

In every harsh and fiery flare,
A message waits with deep repair.
It urges you to seek the truth,
To honor yourself, reclaim your youth.

Listen closely to its call,
It's not a storm to make you fall.
It's a compass pointing true,
To guide you to what you're meant to do.

Learn to make it your closest friend,
A partner on whom you can depend.
It helps you see when paths are wrong,
And guides you to where you belong.

So when you feel its raging heat,
Embrace the wisdom it can meet.
Then gently let it fade away,
As you find a brighter, stronger day.

Anger is the love that fiercely shows,
Where healing starts and freedom grows.
Welcome it, then let it depart,
For it's the voice that guards your heart.

Poem 38

Stop glorifying the endless stride,
The one who battles, never hides,
Who marches on despite the pain,
Through sickness, stress, and grief's disdain.

We praise the ones who push and fight,
Who never rest, who blaze through night,
But true strength lies in something more,
A wisdom that we often ignore.

It's not just in the ceaseless drive,
But in knowing when you need to revive.
In stepping back, in taking pause,
In honoring your body's natural laws.

To rest is not a sign of weakness,
But of a spirit that knows its completeness.
To allow yourself to heal and mend,
Is a mark of strength, a message to send.

When life's demands seem too immense,
And you're overwhelmed by the pretense,
It's brave to admit you need a break,
To step away, for your own sake.

True courage is in the gentle care,
The self-compassion that you wear.
In recognizing that to pause and heal
Is to embrace a strength that's real.

Don't idolize the constant grind,
The relentless pace that leaves you behind.
Instead, honor the moments of retreat,
The quiet strength of a heart that beats.

For in the stillness, wisdom grows,
In tender care, true strength shows.
So cherish the power to take a stand,
To rest, renew, and heal your hand.

True strength is in the quiet grace,
In knowing when to slow the pace.
To give yourself the love you deserve,
Is the bravest act you can observe.

So stop glorifying endless strife,
And embrace the calm within your life.
For in the art of rest and peace,
True strength is found, and burdens cease.

Poem 39

Take a moment, breathe it in,
Celebrate the woman you've always been.
Reflect on the journey, the roads you've paved,
The silent battles, the risks you braved.

You've faced the storms, the trials, the strife,
Overcame obstacles that shaped your life.
With courage fierce and heart so true,
You've navigated paths, both old and new.

The struggles unseen, the tears you've shed,
The hard decisions, the fears you've tread,
Each step you took, though heavy and bold,
Wove the story of a spirit untold.

Celebrate the strength you've found in the fight,
The resilience born from the darkest night.
For every challenge, every heavy load,
Has led you to this place, this road.

You've grown through the pain, evolved through the test,
With a heart full of grace, and courage blessed.
So take a moment, let joy unfold,
In the woman you are, strong and bold.

Raise a glass to the battles won,
To the silent strength that you've become.
Embrace your journey, the scars, the grace,
And celebrate the woman you've come to face.

Poem 40

Sending soft energy to the hearts so grand,
To the women who've fought with strength unplanned.
You've weathered storms with a warrior's might,
In a world that's often a turbulent fight.

Through the trials that marked your days,
In the harshest of nights, in the toughest of ways,
You've stood your ground, faced each storm,
With a spirit that's fierce, and a heart that's warm.

You've borne the weight of each heavy day,
Navigated through shadows that led astray.
With a toughened skin and a will so strong,
You've marched forward, all along.

But now, dear soul, let's shift the view,
From battles won to a softer hue.
For you've earned the peace, the gentle flow,
The calm that's waiting, the grace you'll know.

It's time to let your heart be light,
To dance in the dawn, to embrace the night.
You deserve to glide through life's sweet stream,
To let go of burdens, to live the dream.

Celebrate the strength that's brought you far,
The scars that mark you like a star.
Yet understand, dear one, that you are free,
To flow with ease, to simply be.

The toughness you've shown, the rough exterior,
Was but a shield, a brave barrier.
Now let the softness weave its way,
Into the life you greet each day.

You've fought to survive, but now you're here,
Worthy of peace, of joy, sincere.
So send your spirit to a gentler place,
Where strength meets softness, and life's embrace.

Embrace the quiet moments, the tender grace,
Let the world see your true, serene face.
For you've earned the right to flow and thrive,
In the calm, where your spirit comes alive.

Poem 41

In the quiet dawn of her life's grand play,
A woman stands, come what may.
With a heart that holds the Universe's grace,
And strength etched deep in every place.

Through trials that would make the brave turn cold,
She moves with courage, her story bold.
Her spirit's fire, both fierce and bright,
Guides her through the darkest night.

She's known the weight of life's cruel hand,
Yet she rises, unshaken, to boldly stand.
With a head held high, and eyes that gleam,
She weaves her life, a living dream.

Her love, a beacon through the storm's might,
A guiding star in the dead of night.
Her peace, a sanctuary, calm and true,
A refuge for the heart, a place to renew.

Even when the world around her seems unkind,
She holds a softness, a loving mind.
Her humanity, a light so pure,
A testament to her heart's enduring cure.

She's fought silent battles, fierce and deep,
With a grace that's known, no need to weep.
Each obstacle faced, each hard decision made,
Has shaped the strength in her, unafraid.

So take a moment, let your heart rejoice,
In the woman you've become, let your soul voice.
Celebrate the resilience that you've shown,
The love and peace in you, deeply sown.

For though the storms have tested your will,
You've remained steadfast, unbroken still.
With bold hands, bold heart, and a spirit bright,
You've faced life's trials with endless light.

Your journey's path is a testament grand,
To the strength and love that forever stand.
So honor the woman who's come so far,
A shining beacon, a guiding star.

Embrace the power within your soul,
A spirit that's made you whole.
In every moment, let your strength unfold,
A tale of love and courage, bold.

Celebrate your life, your journey true,
The battles won and the grace you drew.
For you are the embodiment of might and love,
A masterpiece crafted from stars above.

Poem 42

Girls, take time to dream and play,
Go on solo dates, wander and stay,
In quiet cafés, with books in hand,
Build your world like castles in sand.

Wake up early, let the sunrise glow,
Feel the power in each breath you throw,
Work out, dance, feel your heart ignite,
For you alone, chase that morning light.

Buy yourself flowers, tender, divine,
A gift for the soul, your joy, your sign.
Cook your dinner, savor each bite,
A meal crafted by your hands, just right.

This is your life, a canvas bright,
Paint it with love, chase your own light.
Not for their gaze, but for your heart,
Romanticize each moment, make it art.

Poem 43

A strong woman did not wake up one day,
With armor made of steel or words like clay.
She wasn't born with unshakable grace,
But learned to wear resilience on her face.

She walked through fire, through storms untold,
Through nights that chilled her to the bone, cold.
She felt the weight of the world press down,
But never let it steal her crown.

She met betrayal with a silent tear,
Faced her fears, though they whispered near.
The weight of pain didn't make her small,
It built her walls, but not to fall.

She learned to stand when others would flee,
To hold her ground when no one could see,
That every scar, every crack, every fight,
Was a testament to her rising might.

There were days she thought she'd break apart,
Felt the fracture lines inside her heart.
But she picked up the pieces, learned to mend,
And found a strength she didn't intend.

For strength is not born in ease or peace,
It comes when the battles seem to never cease.
It rises when the world's weight is crushing down,
And you still find a way to stand your ground.

A strong woman, she didn't become strong overnight,
But by facing the darkness, embracing the light.
She took all the things meant to tear her apart,
And wove them into the fabric of her heart.

The tears she shed watered the seeds,
Of a strength that grew with every deed.
Her strength, now radiant, was not given for free,
It was earned, forged in adversity.

So when you see her standing tall,
Know it wasn't an easy fall.
She overcame all meant to destroy,
And in doing so, she found her joy.

A strong woman is a story untold,
Of rising again, of being bold.
Not in the absence of pain or strife,
But in embracing it, she found her life.

Poem 44

Be proud of yourself, for the strength you've shown,
For walking through fire, standing alone.
In moments so dark, with no guiding light,
You carried your heart through the endless night.

When others believed you were perfectly fine,
You faced your battles, drew your own line.
Behind every smile, a quiet fight,
Yet you stood tall, never losing your sight.

It would have been easy to let it all go,
To crumble beneath what they'd never know.
But you stayed true, you didn't give in,
You fought for yourself, and you let yourself win.

You are a Queen, in your quiet grace,
With a heart that beats at its own fierce pace.
Remember this always, no matter the pain,
You've crowned yourself through every strain.

For the hardest moments, you passed on your own,
You've built your throne, and your strength has grown.
So wear your crown, let the world see,
The Queen you've become, so wild and free.

Poem 45

Anger, they say, is wild and fierce,
But it's the part of you that holds you near.
It loves you more than you may know,
It burns within, to help you grow.

It rises when your soul feels slight,
When you're mistreated, denied your right.
It's not just fire, it's a gentle guide,
A voice that tells you not to hide.

It knows when you've been cast aside,
Neglected, disrespected, wounded inside.
It whispers first, then roars to say,
"Step away now, don't stay another day."

Your anger sees what you may not see,
That it's time to break from what used to be.
A room, a job, a love gone cold,
Or patterns that no longer hold.

It urges you to leave behind,
The spaces where you feel confined.
To find the light that you deserve,
To walk away with strength, not serve.

Listen close, make anger your friend,
It's not an enemy, nor your end.
It tells you when it's time to go,
And once you listen, it won't need to show.

For anger isn't meant to stay,
It guides you till you find your way.
Then it fades, leaves peace instead,
For you've moved on, lifted your head.

So trust the fire that burns within,
It's there to help, not let you give in.
Embrace its wisdom, heed its call,
Then watch it gently, softly fall.

Poem 46

Ambitious women walk a path so steep,
With dreams to chase and goals to keep.
Their hearts burn bright with endless fire,
Driven by passion, fueled by desire.

But in a world that fears their flame,
They must choose wisely, play the game.
For their journey demands a love that's true,
One that supports all they seek to pursue.

A partner who stands by, not in the way,
Who lifts her higher every day.
Who sees her strength, her power, her drive,
And helps her dreams to come alive.

Or none at all—she'll walk alone,
For her crown is hers, her throne her own.
Better to stand in solitude's grace,
Than dim her light for another's space.

Ambitious women know their worth,
They shape their future, claim the Earth.
And in the end, they will not fall,
For they choose a partner—or none at all.

Poem 47

Hey, woman, hear me clear and true,
You'll never be judged by those who do more than you.
The ones who criticize, who pull you down,
Are the ones afraid of your rising crown.

Their voices echo, but don't you dare fall,
They're doing less, while you give it your all.
So do more for yourself, stand tall and proud,
Rise above the noise, step out from the crowd.

Love yourself with a fierce embrace,
Feed your spirit, set your own pace.
Nourish your soul, let your heart take flight,
In your own strength, reclaim your light.

Let them talk, let them sneer and say,
You'll outgrow their shadows, you'll find your way.
For a woman who loves herself, standing free,
Is a force of nature they'll never be.

Poem 48

Yes, woman, you are a radiant light,
One of the most beautiful souls in sight.
So genuine, pure, yet spicy and bold,
A story untold, a force uncontrolled.

People love you for all that you are—
A breath of fresh air, a blazing star.
You're here to ruffle feathers with flair,
To spark the world, to dare and to care.

You blaze your trails with magic in hand,
Creating wonders, shaping the land.
In every step, in every fight,
You shine with power, your own guiding light.

Never forget the woman within,
The one who dares, who strives to win.
Keep being you, unapologetically free,
For you're the beauty the world longs to see.

Poem 49

A strong woman doesn't beg or plead,
She never stays where she's not freed.
If she feels unwanted, she'll silently know,
And without a word, she'll choose to go.

Her heart, once open, begins to close,
Not out of anger, but because she knows,
That love should flow like a steady stream,
Not be a fight, not be a dream.

She won't stay to fix what's already cracked,
Or chase after feelings that you've pulled back.
Her strength lies in knowing when it's time,
To walk away from a heart's uphill climb.

There's no need for shouting, no need for tears,
She's lived through enough of her own silent fears.
She knows when her presence is more of a weight,
And that's when she'll leave—she won't hesitate.

She'll take her grace, her dignity too,
And leave behind all that she knew.
For she's not one to cling to hope that's faded,
Or wait for a love that's grown outdated.

She won't ask why, she won't demand,
She'll walk away with an open hand.
Not seeking closure, nor wishing ill,
Just silently moving, her spirit still.

She knows her worth, she knows her place,
She's not the one to settle for a second-place race.
So if she feels unwanted, you'll find her gone,
With no trace of the woman who once held on.

For a strong woman loves with all her might,
But she knows when to let go, when to take flight.
She'll turn her back on what doesn't serve,
And walk with the strength she always preserves.

You'll look for her, but she won't be there,
She won't explain, she won't despair.
She'll simply vanish into her own light,
For her strength is in knowing when to fight.

And when to walk, head held high,
Not asking questions, not wondering why.
She won't fix what wasn't meant to be,
She'll just walk away—strong, proud, and free.

Poem 50

Every woman, I believe, must know,
The strength that comes when she's on her own.
No texts, no calls, no hand to hold,
A life where she stands fierce and bold.

She pays her bills, her head held high,
Learns to pamper herself, lets her spirit fly.
Solo dates, long walks, quiet nights,
She builds her world, ignites her lights.

In the stillness, with prayer and grace,
She finds her strength in her own space.
Meditation, reflection, a quiet peace,
She learns to let her worries cease.

For a woman alone is dangerous, you see,
She doesn't cling out of fear to be free.
She knows her worth, she knows her name,
And refuses to play anyone's game.

If she fears being alone, she'll bend and break,
Tolerating things she should never take.
But once she learns to stand her ground,
There's no more fear in being unbound.

Nonsense is something she won't entertain,
She won't settle for heartache or pain.
For a woman who can be alone is strong,
She knows exactly where she belongs.

In solitude, she finds her way,
Her power grows with each passing day.
She'll not tolerate less than she's due,
Because she's learned to love the strength of "just you."

So if she stands alone, let her be,
She's building a fortress no one can see.
And when she steps back into the light,
She's a woman who knows her own might.

Poem 51

Dear females, beautiful and bold,
It's never too late to break the mold.
To begin anew, to dream once more,
To open wide life's untapped door.

Start over again, with courage deep,
Let go of the past that made you weep.
The road ahead is yours to claim,
You're not defined by yesterday's flame.

Start late, if you must, it's never too late,
For time is a myth when you shift your fate.
Every moment is a chance to grow,
To start again, to learn, to know.

Start slow, with patience in your soul,
Every step forward makes you whole.
Life's not a race, there's no set pace,
Just keep moving, with love and grace.

Start again, no matter the fall,
You've risen before, now stand tall.
The world waits for the spark in your eyes,
For the dreams you've yet to realize.

Just start, dear ladies, take the first leap,
Break from the chains that once held you deep.
Your spirit is fierce, your heart is wide,
There's nothing to fear on this new ride.

Stand for yourself, in all that you do,
This life is yours, crafted by you.
Speak your truth, and walk your way,
You're writing your story, starting today.

Start a new life, filled with joy and light,
Leave behind shadows, step into the bright.
The world needs your laughter, your beauty, your grace,
So start again, and find your place.

You are the author of your next page,
No matter your story, no matter your age.
Start over again, as often as needed,
For in every restart, your soul is heeded.

So here's to the beginning, fresh and new,
To the powerful women that live in you.
Start now, start strong, start with all your might,
The future is waiting—go claim your light.